Colonial Settlements in America

Jamestown
New Amsterdam
Philadelphia
Plymouth
St. Augustine
Santa Fe
Williamsburg
Yerba Buena

Philadelphia

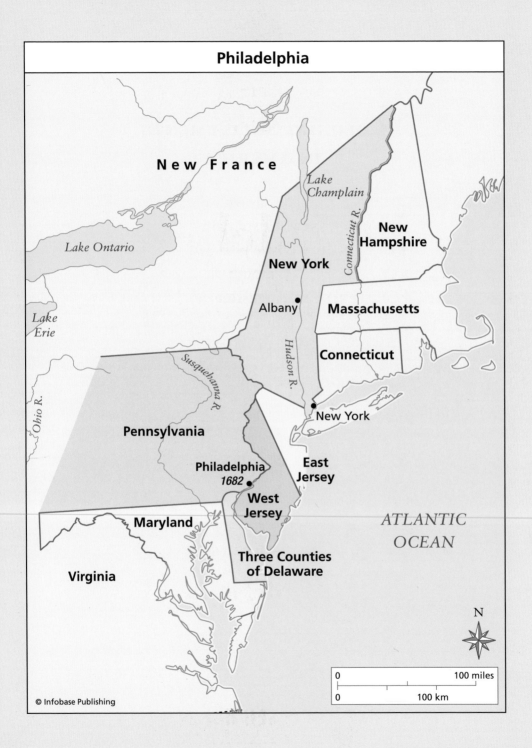

New France

Lake Ontario

Lake Erie

Lake Champlain

New Hampshire

Connecticut R.

New York

Albany

Massachusetts

Connecticut

Susquehanna R.

Hudson R.

Ohio R.

Pennsylvania

New York

East Jersey

Philadelphia
1682

West Jersey

Maryland

Three Counties
of Delaware

Virginia

ATLANTIC OCEAN

N

| 0 | | 100 miles |
| 0 | | 100 km |

© Infobase Publishing

COLONIAL SETTLEMENTS
IN AMERICA

Philadelphia

Shane Mountjoy

SERIES EDITOR

Tim McNeese

CHELSEA HOUSE
PUBLISHERS
An imprint of Infobase Publishing

Frontis: In 1682, William Penn founded the settlement of Philadelphia in the colony of Pennsylvania. Located on the Delaware River, Philadelphia quickly became a center of commerce and trade.

Philadelphia

Copyright © 2007 by Infobase Publishing

Chelsea House
An imprint of Infobase Publishing
132 West 31st Street
New York, NY 10001

ISBN-10: 0-7910-9336-0
ISBN-13: 978-0-7910-9336-8

Library of Congress Cataloging-in-Publication Data
Mountjoy, Shane, 1967-
 Philadelphia / Shane Mountjoy.
   p. cm. — (Colonial settlements in America)
 Includes bibliographical references and index.
 Audience: Grades 7-8.
 ISBN 0-7910-9336-0 (hardcover)
  1. Philadelphia (Pa.)—History—Colonial period, ca. 1600-1775—Juvenile literature. 2. Penn, William, 1644-1718—Juvenile literature. 3. Pennsylvania—History—Colonial period, ca. 1600-1775—Juvenile literature. I. Title. II. Series.
 F158.4.M68 2007
 974.8'1102—dc22   2006028098

Chelsea House books are available at special discounts when purchased in bulk quantities for businesses, associations, institutions, or sales promotions. Please call our Special Sales Department in New York at (212) 967-8800 or (800) 322-8755.

You can find Chelsea House on the World Wide Web at
http://www.chelseahouse.com

Series design by Erika K. Arroyo
Cover design by Ben Peterson

Printed in the United States of America

Bang EJB 10 9 8 7 6 5 4 3 2 1

This book is printed on acid-free paper.

All links and Web addresses were checked and verified to be correct at the time of publication. Because of the dynamic nature of the Web, some addresses and links may have changed since publication and may no longer be valid.

Contents

1

A Meeting of Friends and Neighbors

On a late fall morning in 1682, a small group of people stood outside a small but rapidly growing settlement in present-day southeastern Pennsylvania. The group, made up of white men, stood under a large elm tree, waiting patiently. The men were dressed plainly, in black pants and coats, and white shirts. One of the men wore a blue sash over his coat, as a means of identifying himself as the leader and representative for the rest. This man was William Penn, newly appointed governor of the colony. He and the others were there to meet with the local Native American leaders.

Penn did not believe in wearing flashy clothes, but he wanted to show the Native Americans he was the Englishmen's leader. In wearing the sash, he also demonstrated that he understood their culture. The Native American chiefs wore ceremonial clothing to differentiate themselves from a brave or a leader with lesser authority. Penn believed that if he wore the blue sash, the Native Americans would recognize him

William Penn, depicted here in an engraving by American artist John Sartain, became a Quaker in 1667 at the age of 23. Fourteen years later, King Charles II of England granted Penn a 50,000-square-mile province in America, where members of all faiths were allowed to practice their religion.

as the Englishmen's leader. William Penn hoped to make a lasting peace between the two peoples. Amazingly, the Englishmen standing under the tree were unarmed.

The elm tree was situated in a natural bowl, or amphitheatre. For years, the local Native Americans had used the location as a meeting place. They referred to it as "the place of the kings."[1] Today, it is known as Shackamaxon, an altered form of the Delaware Indian word *Sakimaxing*, which means *place of the kings*. On this day, a group of leaders, including Indian kings, or chiefs, would again meet here to discuss their differences. On this day, William Penn and other leaders of the European settlement planned to meet with Native American leaders and forge an agreement of peace and purchase some land. Although Penn was not a king, the governor did legally own the land and have powers to govern the colony. On this day, Shackamaxon was indeed to be a meeting place for great leaders.

After both groups gathered, a contingent of Native Americans approached the great tree. Chiefs, known as sachems, led the natives. Braves, or warriors, accompanied their chiefs. In sharp contrast to those waiting, the sachems and braves wore brightly colored feathers. Red, yellow, and blue paint decorated their bodies. The Native Americans also carried arms with them—tomahawks, bows, and arrows. Based on appearances, it may have seemed that the two groups had nothing in common. But on this day, the differences did not seem to matter. On this day, the two groups, as different as they were, were meeting to promote the traits they shared in common. Today was a day dedicated to forming lasting friendships.

The Native Americans approached the meeting place. Penn stood at the front and center. Although he was not dressed as royalty, he certainly did not underdress for the occasion. He wore a plain black hat. He was dressed in plain black clothes, with a long coat stretching to his knees. He also wore the blue sash that signified his authority over the other men standing with him. On either side of him were two of his closest advisors and friends, Colonel William Markham and Thomas Pearson. Behind Penn, Markham, and Pearson stood a diverse group of local residents. The group included some of the Europeans who lived in the area: Dutch traders, German farmers, old Swedish veterans dressed in their old-fashioned uniforms, Quakers dressed in their plain clothing, sailors, and laborers. In short, the group looked like a sample of the local community. Penn also had a translator with him, a man named Captain Cockle. Through Cockle, Penn intended to communicate his intentions to the Native Americans.

This was not the first time the Native Americans had heard of Penn. Even before he left England, Penn had written a letter to them many months earlier. In it, the governor pledged his commitment to treating them fairly. He also told them he wanted to live in peace. Below is part of his letter to the Delaware, or Lenni Lenape, who were the dominant tribe of the region:

> My Friends:
>
> There is one great God and power that hath made the world and all things therein to whom you and I and all people owe their being … this great God hath written His law in our hearts by which we are taught to love, help and be good to one another … Now the King of the country where I live hath given me a great province (in your parts of the world). But I desire to enjoy it with your love and consent, that we may always live together as neighbors and friends.
>
> *I am your loving friend,*
>
> WILLIAM Penn[2]

Thus, Penn had already showed the Delawares that he was a man who could be trusted. He had already given them his word that he would treat them as friends and neighbors.

PENNS TREATY with the INDIANS, made 1681 with out an Oath, and never broken. The foundation of Religious and Civil LIBERTY, in the U.S. of AMERICA.

Unlike many of his contemporaries, William Penn not only sought to treat Native Americans equally, but he also expected them to join the community. American artist William Hicks, himself a Quaker, painted this rendition of Penn's famous treaty with the Delaware, or Lenni Lenape, tribe in 1847.

IDENTIFYING WITH THE DELAWARES

When he visited with the Delawares, William Penn tried to place himself within their culture. He learned their language so "that I might not want an interpreter on any occasion."[3] He sat on the ground as they sat. He ate their food and participated in their dances and other rituals. In the words of one historian, "Penn's treatment of the Indians was very modern. He expected them to join in the community; not live in separate reservations. He respected their religion and culture."[4] For the

Delawares, it seems that the English colonists had never sent so good a friend as William Penn.

William Penn was determined to build a new kind of colony. He called it his *holy experiment*, and the basic idea behind it came from his religious beliefs. Penn believed in something Christians call the Golden Rule. It comes from the teachings of Jesus, who taught that each person should treat others the way he or she would like to be treated. The governor wanted to create a society in which people treated each other in ways they wanted to be treated. To do this, he believed that the government needed to treat others with respect. The government of England had treated him poorly. However, Penn believed that, now that he was in charge of the colony's government, he needed to show consideration for others, even if those people disagreed with him. To Penn, this included Native Americans. This is why he attended the meeting at Shackamaxon.

As the meeting began, the Delawares came near the group and Penn warmly welcomed them. The governor made some opening remarks. The sachems listened politely, and then they retreated several yards, out of earshot, to hold a brief discussion. Penn knew this was their custom, so he and his entourage waited patiently. After a few moments, the Delawares returned to Shackamaxon. Taminent, the most important sachem present, led the group. He stopped and placed a simple headdress upon his head. In it was a twisted horn made of metal. This headdress symbolized his power over the other sachems. According to Delaware custom, when a chief wore this headdress, the place and those present became sacred. Thus, to the Delawares, this gathering was a sacred event. Like Penn with his blue sash, Taminent was now identified as the leader of his group because of his headdress.

Taminent sat down on the ground. On either side of him sat the older sachems. Behind this group sat the next-oldest Delawares, in a semicircle. Finally, the youngest warriors sat behind them, forming a third row of the semicircle. After each Delaware had found his place, Taminent then addressed Penn. The chief sachem stated that they were ready to hear what Penn had to say.

Just 38 years old, Penn stood and addressed the Delaware leaders. Despite his young age, Penn was comfortable in these kinds of situations. Reading from a scroll, he told the Delawares that he believed the Great Spirit was father to all men—whether European or Native American. He talked of his dream that all men should live together as friends. He wanted to live in peace with the Delawares, "to do no wrong," and "to serve them in every way."[5]

After reading the treaty aloud to the sachems, Penn laid the scroll down on the ground. As they had done earlier, the Delawares excused themselves to discuss the matter alone. Then, they returned to the meeting and announced to Penn and the others that they accepted his words. They said that the treaty of friendship formed that day was for them and their children. That was the sum of the negotiations. There were no empty rituals carried out to look impressive. No one swore an oath or signed a treaty. The participants did not seal a document with wax and signet rings. Instead, the two sides simply agreed to treat one another as friends and brothers.

The meeting under the great elm was a success. Penn and the Delawares formed a lasting friendship. Both sides had approved of all that had been said. Many years later, the French author Voltaire wrote of the agreement that it was the "only treaty between" whites and Native Americans "which was never sworn to and never broken."[6]

2

Early European Exploration

PORTUGAL

Long before the Delaware Indians met with William Penn
under the great elm tree, Europeans dreamed of establishing colonies in North America and around the world. The story of the founding of Philadelphia has its roots in the establishment and growth of the British Empire. However, it was not England, but Spain and Portugal that were the early leaders of exploration.

In the early fifteenth century, the Portuguese were the first to explore Africa in their attempts to find a trade route with Asia. One influential member of the nobility, known today as Prince Henry the Navigator (sometimes the Seafarer), refined the Portuguese efforts. He earned this name by establishing a school for cartographers and navigators. A cartographer is someone who makes maps. A navigator is someone on a ship who is responsible for planning the journey, as well as knowing the ship's location at all times. Thus, Henry collected all the talent necessary for expanding Portuguese trade by bringing together those who knew the location of a ship with those who knew how to draw coastlines, currents, and so on. Under Henry's leadership, Portugal greatly expanded its colonial presence in Africa. Through its increased access to Africa and the resulting trade routes to the Middle and Far East, Portugal became a wealthy nation. Portuguese success opened the eyes of other European nations to the possibilities of colonialism and trade with Asia. And other nations soon followed the example of Portugal. Leading the way in new exploration was Portugal's neighbor and rival, Spain.

SPAIN

Spain became a major power in the quest for overseas colonies with Christopher Columbus's voyage to the West Indies in 1492. Columbus, who was from Genoa, approached the Spanish with an idea the Portuguese had already rejected: reaching Asia by sailing west, rather than east. Contrary to popular myth, Columbus was not the first to claim the earth was round; many other navigators and explorers at the time held that view. But Columbus did argue that the earth was not as large as what others thought. In fact, Columbus incorrectly calculated the circumference of the earth. He mistakenly used Italian miles for his calculations. (Italian miles are shorter than the miles used for the distances Columbus used to make his calculations—thus his calculations depicted the world as smaller than it really is.) Columbus believed that Asia was much closer to Europe than it actually is. At the end of the fifteenth century, ships of the day could not carry enough food and water to reach Asia.

Navigators and explorers in Spain understood Columbus was probably wrong in his projections, but Spain was a growing nation that was eager to explore. In 1474, King Ferdinand and Queen Isabella had merged the two largest Spanish states of Castile and Aragon under one flag and ruler. The united provinces struggled for control against the Moors, or Spanish

Christopher Columbus's arrival in the West Indies in 1492 opened a period of European exploration and colonization of the New World. Columbus is depicted here bidding farewell to Queen Isabella of Spain before his departure for the New World on August 3, 1492.

Muslims. Ferdinand successfully drove the Moors from the Spanish mainland in 1492. With his country rid of the Muslim threat, Ferdinand wanted to forge his kingdom into a powerful nation. He saw the riches pouring into nearby Portugal from their African trade. Ferdinand knew the experts believed Columbus was wrong. However, Ferdinand believed it was worth a chance to send Columbus in search of a new route to Asia. Fortunately for Spain, the continents of North and South America lay between Europe and Asia. Importantly, the New World was situated almost where Columbus believed Asia to be. Thus, Columbus believed he had found Asia.

Although Columbus was mistaken, he did succeed in help-
ing Spain establish a trade route with the Americas. Spanish
trade with the Americas enriched Spain. Columbus died still
believing he had found a route to the Far East. Spain, however,
quickly formed an empire in the Americas. In time, Spain over-
took Portugal as the European power built on overseas colonies
and trade. Despite Spanish success, another European nation
soon looked toward the Americas as the answer to its colonial
dreams. That nation was England.

ENGLAND

England held many natural advantages over other European
nations in the race to establish and maintain overseas colonies. Perhaps "the most important fact in British history may
well be that Britain is an island."[7] The sea surrounds the island.
The same sea is accessed by every river, cove, and bay along the
coastline. In addition, "No Englishman lives more than 70 miles
from the sea."[8] Easy access to the sea promoted reliance upon
sea trade.

The English Channel separates England from continental
Europe by 24 miles. This separation, though not great, spurred
English reliance on its navy. The English did not need a large
army for defense. Instead, a sound defense required only a strong
navy. Land forces in England only served to limit freedoms, because a king might use armies to reinforce his power. Sea forces
served to protect England from would-be invaders. Indeed, England is a land that encourages its people to sail the seas.

THE FOUNDATION OF AN EMPIRE

Like the Portuguese and Spanish, the seeds of empire were
planted many years before the fruits of colonies were realized.
The foundation for the British Empire began during the reign
of Henry VII, when the first Tudor monarch ruled England

from 1485 to 1509. Henry gained the throne by winning the War of the Roses, a 30-year conflict between two of the great families of England, Lancaster and York. Henry expanded the vision for what the English Navy might accomplish for trade around the globe.

However, it was Henry Tudor's son, the well-known Henry VIII (reigned 1509–1547), who carried out the strategy developed by his father. During Henry VIII's reign, England more than tripled the number of warships in her fleet. England

ENGLISH SEA DOGS

Early English attempts to establish colonies in the New World were often inspired by a motivation less than noble: greed. The thirst for wealth was satisfied through privateers, or sea dogs. Privateers were ship owners or captains who received permission from the British Crown to wage war on enemy ships. Under such authorization, the privateer was allowed to attack ships from another nation and take possession of any cargo. The Crown then received a portion of all plunder. For English privateers, the lure of Aztec gold and silver transported in Spanish ships was a powerful incentive to take to the high seas. Yet, these individuals served a vital function in the development of New World colonies. Sir Francis Drake was perhaps the most famous of these. It was Drake who provided relief to the first Roanoke colony before its demise.

In essence, privateers were nothing more than legalized pirates. Many times, a nation used privateers to create problems for rival nations in the absence of an official declaration of war. Although this seems unwise, it was the accepted system of settling minor disputes throughout the age of exploration. Unfortunately, some privateers did not end their practice of attacking and seizing ships after a war ended. Some of the most well-known pirates from history—including Blackbeard and William "Captain" Kidd—were first sea dogs, legally allowed to seize ships. However, problems with former privateers continued to grow for countries making use of their services.

Finally, European powers decided to establish protections of national sovereignty by setting up international laws. One such agreement was the Declaration of Paris (1856). The countries signing this agreement agreed to outlaw the use of privateers. The United States and other nations initially refused to sign the 1856 Declaration, although the United States did constructed new, larger warships equipped with long-range cannon. Henry also formalized naval administration, creating a formal command structure. Other improvements included creating and building a system of lighthouses and beacons to improve navigation along the coast. England also built newer and larger docks to handle more ships. It is true the English had relied on an effective navy since the days of Alfred the Great, the ninth-century ruler who founded the English Navy. But it was Henry VIII who laid the foundation necessary for England to

honor its terms during the American Civil War (1861–65) and the Spanish-American War (1898). The United States and several other nations finally rejected privateers as a legitimate means of conducting war under the Hague Conferences of 1899 and 1907.

William Kidd (1645–1701) began his career as an English privateer and sea captain, but turned to piracy in the 1690s and was later hanged for his indiscretions. Kidd is depicted here welcoming a woman onboard one of his ships in New York harbor.

achieve later successes as a world power. In fact, it was Henry's vision and innovations for the English Navy that helped Elizabeth I defeat the Spanish Armada in 1588–89, more than 40 years after his death.

EARLY ENGLISH EXPERIENCES WITH COLONIZATION

In the latter years of Henry's reign, England began to reassert its power over nearby Ireland. The English experience in Ireland proved to be influential in a number of ways. First, the English established a policy of colonization. This model for colonizing territory became the standard for future settlements in the New World. Indeed, some of the early figures in establishing North American colonies included men such as Sir Francis Drake, Sir Humphrey Gilbert, and Sir Walter Raleigh (sometimes spelled Ralegh), each of whom had prior experience in English attempts to colonize Ireland.

During the reign of Elizabeth I, Henry's daughter, English naval expertise reached new heights. Sir Francis Drake became only the second man to circumnavigate the globe successfully in a sailing ship (1577–1580). On his journey, Drake landed on the west coast of North America and laid claim to that land for England. Although Drake's discovery and claim did not result in settlement, the English appetite for overseas lands began to grow. Despite Drake's claim on the west coast of North America, it was on the east coast of the continent where future English colonies would be established.

Under Elizabeth, English trade flourished. She further expanded the navy and promoted trade with most of northern Europe from the Netherlands to Russia. The increased trade benefited England's economy. Meanwhile, Spain was busy creating an empire in the New World. Spain's foothold in the New World gave England's enemy an advantage in gaining control

Under King Henry VIII, who reigned from 1509 to 1547, England became a naval power, and would eventually challenge Spain for supremacy in America. In 1536, German Renaissance artist Hans Holbein the Younger became the court painter to Henry VIII and created this famous rendition of the king in 1540.

over the Atlantic shipping lanes. Spanish control, however, proved to be short-lived, as England tried to carve out its own claims in North America.

The first two English attempts at establishing colonies in the New World ended badly. In 1583, Sir Humphrey Gilbert tried to establish a colony in Newfoundland, on the northeastern coast of North America. In 1587, Sir Walter Raleigh made efforts to set up a settlement on the island of Roanoke, off the coast of North Carolina, which he hoped would serve as a base for English privateers who attacked Spanish galleons filled with Aztec riches. Both colonies struggled to survive. The Newfoundland colony suffered from lack of food, bad weather, and poor relations with Native Americans. As for Raleigh's venture, after two attempts to place settlers on the island, the colony of Roanoke disappeared sometime between 1588 and 1590. No one knows for certain what happened to the colonists there.

3

Overseas Growth and Turmoil at Home

Following the disappearance of the Roanoke colony, English adventurers waited more than 15 years before trying again. The next serious attempt made by England was at Jamestown, in 1607. This time, the English succeeded in establishing a permanent settlement. The next successful effort took place in New England when the Pilgrims aboard the *Mayflower* landed at Plymouth (in present-day Massachusetts) in late 1620. The settlers faced many hardships. Yet, the colonists managed to survive and even thrive in North America. Over the next several decades, many Europeans streamed into the colonies. Many of these colonists came to the New World to avoid religious persecution. Others simply came for the opportunity to succeed. Whatever the motivation, the English colonies attracted people from countries throughout Europe.

THE ENGLISH DOMINATE NORTH AMERICA

The English were not the only ones who wanted to establish colonies in North America. The Netherlands, or Holland, also

23

While sailing along the Atlantic coast aboard his ship *Half Moon* in 1609, Henry Hudson arrived at the mouth of the river that would later bear his name. Although Hudson did not discover a northwest passage to the Pacific Ocean, his descriptions of a land rich with timber and game persuaded the Dutch to colonize the region that would later become New York.

had colonies there. In 1609, an Englishman named Henry Hudson sailed into what is now New York Harbor for the Dutch East India Company. He sailed up the river that later was named for him. Hudson's descriptions of the land rich with timber and game persuaded the Dutch to establish a colony there. In 1621, the Dutch West India Company was created. This was done in order to colonize the region Hudson initially explored 12 years earlier. The French and English, who also traded in the area, disputed Dutch claims, but the company was organized enough to set up a colony, called New Netherland. Within the colony lay the city of New Amsterdam, now called New York City. The primary Dutch settlement lay on the coast. But Dutch settlers ventured west, and some even settled at the site that later became Philadelphia.

Over time, the English began to view the Dutch colonists as more than just unwelcome neighbors. Instead, the English saw the Dutch as dangerous competitors. In 1651, Parliament passed the Navigation Act. This law "required that the owner, master, and a majority of the crew of any ship bearing exports from England's colonial possessions be English."[9] The law placed the same restrictions on goods imported to the English colonies. In other words, the English attempted to drive the Dutch traders out of business. As one might expect, the Dutch were unhappy with such restrictions. The two countries ended up fighting a series of wars over the issue, with the First Anglo-Dutch War lasting from 1652 to 1654. William Penn's father served with distinction in the English Navy during this conflict. Holland lost the war and agreed to recognize the Navigation Act at the Treaty of Westminster.

Although fighting between the two nations was halted for the time being, England and Holland still jostled for position throughout the 1650s. At first, England appeared to be at a disadvantage. The English very much wanted to become a greater trade power with many colonies, but the Dutch stood in the way of English plans. The Dutch possessed a worldwide system of established trade routes. Dutch traders were the only ones permitted to trade with Japan. The Dutch were rapidly becoming a threat to the future growth of English trade.

King Charles II recognized the Dutch threat. He authorized English forces to bring New Amsterdam under English control. On August 26, 1664, the Dutch awoke to find four English warships anchored offshore. The English asked for a peaceful surrender, and promised to give the Dutch colonists equal rights within a new English colony. The Dutch governor, Peter Stuyvesant, stalled for time. He hoped that the company would send reinforcements to fight the English. The English force waited patiently, knowing the Dutch colonists had little choice. In the end, Stuyvesant was forced to surrender the Dutch colony to the English. On September 8, 1664, Governor Stuyvesant signed the necessary paperwork, handing control of the colony over to England. Charles gave the land to his brother James, the Duke of York. Both the city and colony were renamed in his honor: New Amsterdam became the city of New York and New Netherland was renamed the colony of New York. Unfortunately, the land grant to James did not clearly specify the boundaries of the colony. This was a common problem in many of the early colonial charters. The unclear boundaries led to many disagreements, including the exact boundary with Pennsylvania.

THE ENGLISH COLONIAL SYSTEM: A JUMBLED APPROACH

The English established three types of colonies in North America: royal, charter, and proprietary. In a royal colony, the ruling monarch preserved control of the colony and ruled it through appointed officials. Georgia, South Carolina, North Carolina, Virginia, New Jersey, New York, Massachusetts, and New

Beginning in 1624, the Dutch-controlled colony of New Netherland was centered around what is today New York City, but it spread south to Cape Henlopen in southern Delaware and east to Cape Cod. However, by the time Peter Stuyvesant (depicted here) became director general of the Dutch colony in 1647, English colonists were already claiming Dutch territory for themselves.

Hampshire were all royal colonies. Some of these royal colonies began as charter or proprietary colonies, only to see monarchs reassert control for a variety of reasons. Such colonies usually remained under royal control and operated as royal colonies. Charter colonies were established when the king or queen signed a document or charter to a group of settlers, authorizing them to govern the colony. Only Connecticut and Rhode Island were founded as charter colonies. Finally, proprietary colonies were established when the monarch issued a charter and land to a proprietor or private owner. The proprietor was permitted to govern the colony, because the colony legally belonged to the individual. Maryland, Delaware, and Pennsylvania were each proprietary colonies. Over time, the Crown sought to strengthen its power over the colonies, and most of the colonies were rechartered as royal colonies. Pennsylvania, however, legally remained in the Penn family until the Declaration of Independence was signed in 1776 and a state constitution was adopted.

THE ENGLISH CIVIL WAR

Beginning in 1642, a series of conflicts within England erupted between the Crown and Parliament. This struggle became known as the English Civil War. Tensions arose from differences in opinion over two different, yet closely related arguments: politics and religion. The first centered on the powers and role of the king and Parliament. The other highlighted religious differences within England.

The political differences in English society were plain to see, yet difficult to overcome. Essentially, King Charles I wanted to rule as an absolute monarch, or by divine right. According to this philosophy, a king rules because God placed him on the throne. Thus, all subjects should obey him with absolute loyalty. Unfortunately for Charles, there were many in Parliament who believed that the elected representatives serving in the House of Commons were the ones who had the right to govern.

The religious differences contributing to the war stemmed from the role of the Church of England. In 1534, King Henry VIII led the English Church in separating from the leadership and authority of the Roman Catholic Church. At that time, the Church became known as the Church of England, or the Anglican Church. Under Henry, the monarch served as head of the Church in England. On the other hand, Charles I

CAVALIERS AND ROUNDHEADS

The English Civil War tore friends and families apart. Divided loyalties to either the king or Parliament separated one Englishman from another. Others disagreed over the role of religion in English society. Usually, supporters of the British Crown were Catholic or at least supported religious rights for Catholics. Those backing Parliament also defended the position of the Church of England as the official state religion. Thus, different views on religion and politics divided English society.

Interestingly, there was another distinct difference separating the two sides in the English Civil War—their haircuts. Supporters of Parliament were nicknamed *Roundheads* from the style of haircut many of them wore: long hair on the top of the head, with the sides and back either cut very short or shaved. The Roundheads did not cover the sides or back of their heads with hair, thus exposing their *round heads*. The supporters of the king were called Cavaliers, or Royalists. These men wore their hair long in back and on the sides. The differences between the two hairstyles could not be more pronounced.

The term *Roundhead* first appeared in late 1641. Royalists noted that many supporters of Parliament wore their hair in an undignified manner. While the conflict raged throughout the 1640s, the name *Roundhead* was used to mock supporters of Parliament. In fact, to use the name in Parliament's army resulted in punishment! Despite its initial derogatory intent, the nickname stuck. Roundhead continued to be used as a way of identifying supporters of the Parliament, or self-government, until William and Mary ascended to the throne at the conclusion of the Glorious Revolution in the late 1680s.

William Penn, the founder of Philadelphia, wore his hair in the fashion of a Cavalier. Thus, the dissenting Quaker was often accused of being a Royalist and favoring Catholic rights. Ironically, Penn believed in the ability of people to govern themselves, hardly the position of a Royalist. He also supported the rights of all individuals to practice religion according to personal convictions. Therefore, the founder of Philadelphia presents a complicated picture: he held the religious views and wore his hair like a Cavalier, yet he dressed simply and held many of the political views of a Roundhead concerning self-government.

favored an approach that steered the Church toward the beliefs of the Catholic Church. For many in England, this was unacceptable. The result was a long and bloody civil war.

4

The Penn Family

WILLIAM PENN THE ELDER: ADMIRAL AND HERO

William Penn, the father of the man who eventually established Pennsylvania, gave his name to his son. Despite sharing the same name, the father and son were very different people. The younger Penn became a devout Quaker, pursuing a life of peacemaking and improving conditions for his fellow citizens. In contrast, the senior Penn made his reputation in battle, where he served as a captain in the Royal Navy during the English Civil War, eventually attaining the rank of admiral. The English Civil War was essentially a fight between King Charles I and those who believed in the king's power and those who believed in the power of Parliament. Those who supported the king were called Royalists. Those who supported Parliament also happened to be Puritans, a group within the Church of England that wanted to see the church "purified" of some of its remaining Catholic features. The elder Penn tended to favor the monarchy during the conflict, although he desperately wanted to

William Penn's father, Sir William Penn (1621–1670), was a prominent figure in the English Navy. He achieved great success during the First Anglo-Dutch War (1652–54), winning several battles against the Dutch, which led to his promotion to admiral. The elder Penn is depicted in this 1660s oil painting by Dutch artist Sir Peter Lely.

serve in the navy, regardless of who held the reins of national power. Thus, Penn did not fully commit to either side. Instead, he simply obeyed his orders, no matter who was in charge of the government. Some historians characterize the elder Penn as a moderate. That is, Penn supported Parliament, but he also believed in the powers of the king. Once Parliament gained control of the navy, Penn still continued to serve as an admiral.

The civil war caused problems for many families in England. To insulate his family from the strife and turmoil, Penn moved them from London to a large house about 10 miles outside the city in the parish of Wanstead. The country estate afforded the younger Penn opportunities to enjoy the outdoors, explore nearby forests, and raise a variety of animals.

While the Penn family enjoyed a quiet life at Wanstead, Penn the father was moving up through the ranks. Following the end of the civil war, the English fought against the Dutch in a conflict known as the First Anglo-Dutch War (1652–54). Exclusively a naval contest, the war began over disagreements related to trade between the two countries and their overseas colonies. Penn was an able captain, securing several victories in battle over the Dutch. His successes in war led to his appointment to admiral in the English Navy.

In 1654, the elder Penn left to serve in the war against Spain. Admiral Penn distinguished himself as an able commander, but he failed to capture Hispaniola, a major island of the Spanish American colonies. When he returned to England in late summer 1655, Oliver Cromwell dismissed Penn from the navy. Then, Cromwell imprisoned him in the Tower of London. Penn suffered there for five weeks. Finally, Cromwell's anger faded, and he ordered Penn's release.

William Penn the elder realized his tenuous position. Fearing the government might again take action against him, Penn decided to focus his energies on his landholdings in Ireland, where the Penn family soon moved. Later, the political climate changed in England, and the former admiral regained his commission and served in the navy for England.

THE RETURN OF THE MONARCHY

After the execution of Charles I in 1649, Parliament ruled England. Some still saw the need for a chief executive, but many did not want a king. Instead, in 1653, Parliament installed the leader of the Puritans, Oliver Cromwell, as the Lord Protector. Cromwell was king in every way except name, although he did respect the power of Parliament. When Cromwell died in 1658, his son Richard was then named Lord Protector. Whereas Oliver was an effective leader, his son was not. Within two years, many members of Parliament decided that Richard Cromwell was incapable of governing. Many wanted the royal family of the Stuarts to return to rule England.

Therefore, in 1660, Parliament asked Charles, the oldest son of Charles I, to return from his exile in France and serve as king. Charles accepted the offer. Parliament sent Admiral Penn with 31 ships to escort the monarch back to England. When Penn arrived in France, Charles knighted the admiral. Admiral Penn was now Sir William Penn. Charles was crowned king, and he began ruling as Charles II.

Shortly after Charles returned to England, Parliament passed a law requiring all citizens to worship according to the rules of the Church of England. Those who did not faced harsh punishment. William Penn, now a student at Oxford, saw dissenters such as Puritans and Quakers mistreated. Sometimes the dissenters were attacked with rocks. Sometimes authorities placed the dissenters in jail. The idea that people should be able to follow their own religious convictions began to take hold in William.

THE YOUNG FOUNDER

The story of Philadelphia begins long before a Quaker purchased land from Native Americans on the banks of the Delaware River. The story of Pennsylvania's great city cannot be told without telling the story of its founder, William Penn. Penn was born on

As a young child, William Penn attended Chigwell School, which is depicted here in a woodcut. Although Penn studied many subjects, including Latin and Greek, at the preparatory school in Wanstead, Essex, his most important discovery was religion.

October 24, 1644, in London. At age three, young William was stricken with smallpox. Although he survived, William's father decided to move his family out of the city into a country house in Wanstead (also insulating them from the tumultuous political situation).

When he was old enough, his parents sent him to a preparatory school called Chigwell. While there, he studied Latin and Greek, which he later knew quite well. He attended Chigwell School until he was about 12 years old. Then, due to the political climate that endangered his father, Penn's family moved to their family estate in Ireland. There, the ex-admiral hired a tutor to continue young William's education.

The move away from England proved to have a major impact on the boy's life. Although he first discovered religion at Chigwell, it was in Ireland that young William Penn first heard the English preacher Thomas Loe—a Quaker. Loe spoke of an "inner light" inside each person, a light that guided one through life. Penn was moved by the preaching and later chose to become a Quaker. This newfound influence changed Penn's life, which eventually led him to establish a colony in North America.

COLLEGE AT OXFORD

After returning to London, Penn entered the Christ Church College at Oxford on October 26, 1660. He was admitted as a "gentleman commoner."[10] His time at college was turbulent. During his second year, William began regularly attending religious lectures off campus. These lectures were held in the home of Dr. John Owen, a Puritan preacher. Owen preached tolerance of people who believed differently than the established church. Penn took Owen's words to heart, and put his own beliefs into practice. In violation of school rules, William refused to go to the required chapel services of the Church of England held at Oxford. The college rebuked him, but William still refused to participate in the services. Finally, college authorities expelled him in March 1662.

Following his rather brief college experience at Oxford, Penn's father sent the young man to France, in order to further his son's education. Young Penn toured France and then attended Saumur, the highly touted Protestant university. There, William learned even more about following his own conscience. He came to believe more fully in religious liberty and in the freedom to obey his own sense of right and wrong. After completing his studies, William visited Italy for a time, before his father sent for him. Once home, Penn began studying law in June 1664 at Lincoln's Inn, one of London's four legal associations. (Lawyers or aspiring lawyers were required to belong to a legal association in order to learn and practice law.)

PENN THE QUAKER

In 1665, an outbreak of the plague in London forced Penn and his family to their country estate. Before they left, however, Penn witnessed a group of people acting on their beliefs: the Quakers, or the Religious Society of Friends. The religious group began in England in the 1650s. At that time, there were many different groups within Christianity. Each claimed to know better than the other groups how to live, which practices to keep or exclude, and which beliefs should be emphasized. People who were unhappy with the disunity within Christianity helped start the Society of Friends. These early leaders included a man named George Fox, whom many credit with founding the Quakers. Others were also involved, but Fox certainly was the most significant individual in the early years of the movement. His teachings about loving others helped define early Quakerism.

The Quakers were persecuted at the hands of the government and most of English society. But these same Quakers did all they could to ease the suffering of those afflicted with the plague. The images of a mistreated group reaching out to help others greatly affected Penn.

The following spring, the admiral sent young William to manage affairs on the family estate in Cork, Ireland. Penn remained in Ireland for about a year and a half, before returning to London in December 1667. However, the time spent in Ireland was both significant and influential for the young man now in his early twenties. Penn sought out and listened to the Quaker preacher he had first heard a decade before: Thomas

While he was growing up, George Fox was very religious but yearned to find a means to express his devotion to God. He found his answer by turning inward and discovering that God could be found within the soul of each person. In 1647, at the age of 23, Fox began spreading his new beliefs in what became known as Quakerism.

Loe. Penn became convinced that the Quaker ways were for him. He attended meetings of the Friends and was arrested at one such meeting in 1667. Soon after his release, Penn returned to London.

PENN THE RELIGIOUS WRITER

Once home, Penn openly and enthusiastically identified himself with the Friends. His father was not happy about William's decision to become a Quaker. The two argued about it, but could not reach an agreement. Finally, the admiral threw his son out of the house. Young William was forced to live with other Quakers willing to take him in.

But his personal hardships did not discourage him. Instead, Penn began speaking out for the rights of Quakers. He began writing pamphlets to explain the Quaker ways. In 1668, he published *The Sandy Foundation Shaken*. As with all religious pamphlets published at the time, Penn did not get a royal license for the publication. However, the Quakers were unlike virtually all other religious groups within English society. Some officials believed that Penn's tract promoted dangerous ideas that threatened the Church of England. Consequently, authorities arrested Penn and placed him in the Tower of London in the fall of 1668, where his father had been imprisoned 13 years earlier.

IN PRISON

The time spent in the Tower proved to be crucial for William Penn. Authorities tried to intimidate the 24-year-old into taking back some of the things he had written. They offered to release him if he would only retract some of his statements. Penn refused to be swayed. Instead, he declared, "My prison shall be my grave before I will budge a jot; for I owe my conscience to no mortal man."[11] His time spent in the Tower stiffened his determination to stand up for individual rights of religious conviction.

Penn's resolve placed the royal family in a thorny situation. Charles II and his brother James (later James II) counted the Penn family among their friends. Both Charles and James would gladly release William, if only he would recant his earlier statements. Convinced of the rightness of his cause, Penn refused.

Although he would not recant, a friend convinced Penn to explain his views more clearly. While still a prisoner, Penn took

THE TOWER OF LONDON

The Tower of London is a prominent and historic landmark located in central London. The "Tower" is actually several buildings situated on the River Thames. Due to their location on the river, these buildings have been used for a variety of purposes over time, including use as armories, observatories, offices for storing public records, palaces, a royal mint, a royal treasury, walled fortresses, and the buildings even housed a zoo. However, the Tower was best known as a prison and place for public executions. Its use as a prison, especially for members of the upper class, generated the phrase "sent to the Tower" to mean imprisoned.

The most easily recognizable part of the structure is the White Tower, a square building with turrets or little towers on each corner. The building is named for these turrets. The White Tower stands on the site where the Roman Emperor Claudius erected a fortress to protect the Roman settlement there. William I ordered the White Tower constructed in 1078, and Richard the Lionheart had a moat dug around it.

Many notables spent time imprisoned in the Tower. Perhaps the most famous of its occupants was Elizabeth I, who was imprisoned there during the reign of her half sister Mary. Eventually, Elizabeth won her release and later assumed the throne upon Mary's death. Others were not so lucky. The Tower grounds were the site of the execution of Thomas More in 1535 and two wives of Henry VIII—Anne Boleyn in 1536 and Catherine Howard in 1542. Other famous occupants who met their end on the Tower grounds include George the Duke of Clarence, the brother of Edward IV. William Shakespeare embellished the details surrounding George's death, depicting the duke being drowned in a large barrel of wine within the Tower.

Today, lacking any military or official purpose, the Tower is primarily a tourist attraction. The buildings are still classified as a royal residence, although no member of the royal family lives there. Instead, the buildings boast a display of armor from the Royal Armouries, dating back to William the Conqueror, who took control of England in 1066. The Yeoman Warders, or Beefeaters, provide both ceremonial and real security. The warders provide

up his quill to write another tract. This document put in plain words Penn's views, which led to his imprisonment. The tract— *No Cross, No Crown*—did not take back anything printed earlier. However, the royal family could now claim that the young

services as tour guides and perform the nightly ritual called the Ceremony of the Keys, when the gates of the Tower are formally locked, a tradition that began in 1340.

In 1668, William Penn was arrested and imprisoned in the Tower of London. Pictured here is the Middle Tower, which was built in the thirteenth century and guards the outer perimeter entrance of the Tower complex.

man had come to his senses and deserved to be pardoned. In July 1669, Penn was finally released, after nearly nine months in the Tower, with no charges ever filed against him. Instead of breaking his will, the experience served to harden his resolve in the cause for religious liberty.

5

Fighting for Religious Freedom

After William Penn was released from the Tower of London in 1669, he faced a hostile religious climate. Charles II wanted Parliament to allow Catholics more religious freedom, while Parliament wanted to limit any religious group other than the Church of England. Parliament passed a law outlawing other religious groups from meeting and non-Anglican clergy from preaching. William Penn and other Quakers still went to their meetinghouse, only to find it locked up by the government. Penn decided to preach outside the meetinghouse. Officials arrested him and another Quaker, Captain William Meade, for disturbing the peace.

What followed was one of the most important court cases in the history of England. The trial began on September 3, 1670. The judges did all they could to unnerve the two men. When Penn and Meade entered the courtroom, they followed the Quaker custom of leaving their hats on. This violated courtroom etiquette, and one of the attending officers rudely knocked their hats from their heads. Penn and Meade ignored

In 1670, William Penn and fellow Quaker William Meade were arrested by English officials for disturbing the peace, because they had held a religious meeting outside their meetinghouse. Despite pressure from the judges who presided over the trial (depicted here), the jury refused to convict Penn and Meade, and they were eventually cleared of all charges.

the insult and stood respectfully before the bench. One of the judges roared at the defendants, demanding them to put their hats on. The two stood silently, and the offending officer placed the hats back on the men's heads.

Now the judge demanded they remove their hats. Penn and Meade explained that, although they meant no disrespect, they did not believe in removing their hats to show respect. One of the judges then declared the two to be in contempt of court and fined them for wearing their hats in the courtroom. Penn matter-of-factly observed that they first entered the courtroom without their hats. If they wore their hats, it was "by order of the Bench; and therefore not we, but the Bench should be fined."[12] The judges ignored him and swore in the jury.

The case was then revealed to be a poorly constructed argument against Penn and Meade. Witnesses swore they saw the two men outside the meetinghouse. Some testified that Penn spoke there, but no one actually heard what it was he said. After establishing only that Penn and Meade were present outside the meetinghouse, and that Penn was speaking there, the panel of judges demanded the two enter a plea. Penn and Meade asked the court to explain the charges to them. This led to a vigorous debate over what law they might have broken.

The judges soon lost all patience with the two defendants. Repeated attempts to silence the two failed. Finally, Penn was placed in the "bale-dock—a well-like place at the farthest end of the court, in which he could neither see nor be seen."[13] Despite his situation, Penn continued to ask questions of the judges. Captain William Meade followed the example of Penn and asked them to explain the nature of the charges. The judges' patience was now at an end, and Meade soon joined Penn in the bale-dock.

Next, the judges turned their wrath toward the jury. The panel of judges insisted that the jurors bring back a guilty verdict; no other verdict was acceptable. The judges even threatened the jury if they did not return with a guilty verdict, telling them that to do so would be "at your own peril."[14] When Penn heard these instructions, he called out from the bale-dock, questioning the legality of threatening a jury in order to get a desired verdict.

The judges mocked Penn, claiming they could not hear one who could not be seen. Penn responded by reminding them they had removed him to the bale-dock. The judges angrily ordered Penn and Meade removed from the proceedings.

During their trial, William Penn and William Meade were forced to spend time in London's most infamous prison, Newgate. The prison housed criminals from 1188 to 1902 and is depicted in many works of literature, including Charles Dickens's novels *Great Expectations* and *Oliver Twist*.

Officers placed the two defendants in the worst cell in Newgate, the worst prison in London. Newgate was well known as a disgusting jail. Penn described Newgate as smelling so bad "that the Lord Mayor would think it unfit for pigs to lie in."[15]

The judges again instructed the jury to reach an acceptable verdict—that is, one acceptable to the judges—and the 12 jurors left to deliberate. After an hour and a half, the jury returned to the courtroom. They announced that they could not agree on a verdict. The judges sent them out again. After lengthy discussions, the jury returned. This time, the members of the jury were in complete agreement: They would only state that William Penn was guilty of speaking in public. When pressed as to whether or not the speaking took place at an unlawful assembly, the jury stood firm.

The judges, now quite angry, threatened the jury further, telling the 12 men that only a guilty verdict was acceptable to the court. One judge declared, "Gentleman, you shall not be dismissed until you bring in a verdict which the court will accept. You shall be locked up, without meat, drink, fire, and tobacco."[16] Then, he told them, "We will have a verdict by the help of God, or you shall starve for it."[17]

Penn, back in the court chambers for what was supposed to have been the reading of the verdict, protested this treatment of the jury. "My jury," he claimed, "ought not to be thus menaced."[18] And he insisted that "their verdict should be free—not forced."[19] Despite Penn's objections, the jury was forced to spend the night cold, hungry, and thirsty, while they deliberated about a verdict they had already given. The scene was repeated the next day, even though it was a Sunday. Again, the jury endured another night with nothing to eat or drink, and no fire to warm themselves.

However, on the third day of the trial, the jury held firm to their earlier decision. In the face of threats and fines from the judges, the 12 men bravely stood up for the rights of William Penn and Captain Meade. After presenting their decision, the court held each member of the jury and the two defendants in contempt of court. Officials sent the 14 men back to Newgate.

Penn intended to stay in prison rather than pay his fine. However, an anonymous friend paid the fines of both Penn and

Meade, securing their release just two days later. For Penn, although he did not want the fine paid, the gesture came at a critical time: His father was at home, dying. William Penn rushed home to see the ailing admiral. The two made their peace with one another. As the admiral lay dying, he continued to think of his son. Sir William sent messages to both King Charles and his brother James, Duke of York, asking each to treat his Quaker son kindly. Both responded with kind words for the dying man. James even agreed to act as guardian and protector to young William. Thus, the seeds were sown that led to an unlikely friendship between an heir to the throne and a dissenting son of a naval hero.

Eleven days after the trial, Admiral Penn died at his home. William Penn, as eldest son, inherited his father's entire estate. The Quaker who had followed his convictions and refused to let the government intimidate him now owned a great deal of land that yielded a substantial annual income. With a guaranteed income, Penn was able "to preach and publish widely, and to

THE BUSHEL CASE

After Penn and Meade won their case, the fight for liberty continued. The judges had ordered the jury to find the two Quakers guilty. However, the jury found the two men not guilty. The court then held the jury in contempt of court and fined them. Each of the jurors was sent to Newgate Prison, where they were to remain until their fines were paid. One member of the jury, Edward Bushel, refused to pay the fine. Then, from prison, he filed a lawsuit against the court.

Taking his case to the Court of Common Pleas, Bushel argued that the court's actions against him violated his rights as an Englishman. Bushel believed the court acted improperly when it tried to pressure the jury. The Court of Common Pleas agreed with Bushel, stating that judges are not to intimidate a jury. The Bushel case, which grew out of Penn's trial, helped establish the independence of juries. This principle later became a key feature of the American court system.

contribute generously to the aid of the Persecuted Quakers," as well as support Quaker mission efforts.[20] More importantly, Penn also inherited the right to collect repayment of a large loan his father had made to the king. Moreover, this loan, once it was paid, would forever change the course of colonial settlements in England's American colonies.

MARRIAGE

After the Penn-Meade trial, William Penn did not stop speaking out on behalf of religious liberties. Instead, he grew bolder. Five months later, Penn found himself back in Newgate Prison. This time, he was accused of unlawful assembly. He also was in trouble for refusing to swear an oath against taking up arms against the king. Because Quakers reject violence and even refuse to carry arms, this charge seems ridiculous. Although the charges made little sense, Penn spent six months in prison before winning his freedom. Upon his release, Penn traveled to Holland and Germany, where he organized Quaker meetings. He then returned to England.

On April 4, 1672, William Penn married Gulielma Springett, the stepdaughter of a well-known Quaker named Isaac Penington. Quaker weddings are simple ceremonies. No minister performs the rites. Instead, the groom and his bride state their vows to each other. Each promises to love the other and to be faithful for the rest of his/her life. Then, there is a period of silent meditation. After a while, others may stand up and offer words of encouragement to the couple. After that, the couple is considered married.

THE NEED FOR A QUAKER HAVEN

While a newlywed, Penn listened to George Fox, who spoke at a series of meetings. Fox, one of the founders of the Quaker movement, had recently returned from a trip to America. There, he found a growing population of Quakers. Fox preached about the opportunities to follow one's own conscience in America. Penn listened to Fox, and began to dream about opportunities for Quakers in America.

William Penn envisioned a better life for himself and fellow Quakers—a life in which individuals could practice their religious beliefs without interference from government authorities. He knew there was abundant land in North America. Perhaps he could use his connections to secure land across the Atlantic. Then, he could establish a colony in which people could follow their own religions rather than be subjected to government mistreatment. Such a colony could become a place of safety for Quakers and other dissenters.

6

Penn's Woods

William Penn decided that the Quakers needed a place where they could practice their religious beliefs in freedom. Penn did not want the government telling them how to worship. He called his idea for such a place a *holy experiment*. But this kind of experiment had never before been done. England already had an official church, the Church of England, sometimes called the Anglican Church. England also had many laws that made it hard for people to worship differently from the Anglicans. Besides, in England, a man born into poverty was likely to spend his whole life in poverty. And a man born into wealth was likely to spend his whole life in wealth. English society was too divided between the rich and poor.

In 1680, Penn became convinced that the best chance for creating a society in which Quakers could live freely was in the New World. Using imagery of a snake, he described how he did not believe his native country could be transformed into a place that accepted Quakers for who they were. "There is no hope for England," he wrote, "the deaf adder cannot be charmed."[21] "At length his mind began to fix itself on what he called the Holy Experiment of planting a religious democracy in the western world."[22]

Penn made up his mind that England was not the place to try his holy experiment. Instead, a place far away from England was needed, to give the experiment a chance to succeed. All that was needed was a place. Penn did not have a place, at least not yet. But he did have a valuable asset: The king of England owed him a large sum of money.

Penn's dream of a colony based on religious freedom was a bold vision. The land he asked for was a wilderness. There were few settlers there. The only Europeans living there were not

THE BRITISH SYSTEM OF PEERAGES

English peerages reinforce the social system that separates people by rank. William Penn did not believe in such artificial barriers between people. He was determined to prevent such a system from developing in his colony. Perhaps it was Penn's experiences as a dissenter and the resulting persecution he suffered at the hands of the nobility that caused him to distrust those who gained titles through favors from the monarch or through birth. Whatever his motivations, Penn insisted on equal rights in his colony, thereby avoiding some of the complications arising from a peerage system.

How was the English peerage system set up? There were five ranks of peers: duke, marquess, earl, viscount, and baron. "Duke" comes from the Latin word dux, which means leader. "Mark," a Germanic word, means border and hints at the idea of an established border. The word and title eventually became marquess—similar to the French rank marquis—and simply means a marked border. "Earl" comes from the Anglo-Saxon eorl, which stands for a freeborn military leader. "Count" is a title of nobility commonly used throughout Europe, and holds virtually the same meaning as earl. A viscount, from the Latin vicecomes, is a vice-count, thus one step below the earl, which is equal to a count. Last of all, "baron" traces its roots from the old German word baro, which means freeman.

Although there are five different ranks of peers, there are only two different kinds of peerages: lifetime and hereditary. A lifetime peerage is an

English, but either Dutch or Swedish. The Swedes were mostly farmers. The Dutch also farmed, but some of them also engaged in trade, supplying the other Europeans with necessary goods from Europe. Most of the settlers living there had not even built houses. The few standing houses were primitive structures made of wood, with straw or reeds covering the roof in place of shingles. Such roofs are known as thatched roofs. The rest of the settlers lived in even more primitive dwellings. In other words, the young colony was undeveloped. However, the lack of a large established society is exactly what Penn required for his holy experiment. He wanted to be able to create fresh traditions in a new and unspoiled world. A land with hardly any Europeans,

honor often conferred upon an individual for his or her service to the country or for outstanding contributions to a particular field. Traditionally, the British Crown awards such peerages to principal office holders when they retire, such as the prime minister or the Archbishop of Canterbury. Others might receive lifetime peerages upon the nomination of the political parties in Parliament. As a matter of practice, lifetime peers are usually granted the rank of baron or baroness, but the decision is made by the monarch. Such peers might be appointed to serve within the judicial system, but most are simply named as a means of bestowing honor upon a well-deserving individual.

A hereditary peer is a position of nobility that is inherited. As long as there are surviving descendants of a hereditary peer, such a peerage continues to exist. Once the last descendant dies, the peerage ends. Historically, hereditary peerages could also be lost by committing treasonable offenses. However, the Crown could and sometimes did restore title and rank to individuals. These peerages are granted from the king or queen, and are usually passed on to the oldest son. Sometimes, the monarch may spell out other means of inheriting the peerage, although most pass through a male relative. Until 1999, all hereditary peers were permitted to sit in the House of Lords. Today, only 92 peers may sit in the chamber, and other peers elect all but 2.

few settlements, and the potential for successful cities seemed altogether perfect for his vision.

PETITIONING THE KING

In May 1680, William Penn petitioned the king for a large tract of land. He asked for this land, because the king owed his family a lot of money. In fact, the king owed Penn money and a peerage. A peerage is the structure of titles of nobility in England. A peer was one who held a title of nobility. These ranks include the following: duke, marquess, earl, viscount, and baron. Penn was entitled to become Viscount Weymouth. Penn was also entitled to receive payment of the loan his father once gave the king. Charles did not have enough money to repay the Penn family. Worse still, the king could earn money by conferring a title of nobility—like Viscount Weymouth—on someone who would then pay the king. In other words, the king could sell the peerage. Since Charles owed Penn money and a peerage, Penn could get both without paying anything to the king. Charles wanted to pay off his debt, but he did not have the money to do so.

King Charles faced a tough choice. His brother James, Duke of York, owned the land Penn wanted. James did not want to give up the land that the English had acquired from the Dutch (including present-day New York, Delaware, and Pennsylvania). James had only recently acquired the land that later became Pennsylvania, along with a great deal of other property in North America.

THE SEED OF A NATION

On March 4, 1681, Charles II granted a land charter to William Penn for a large tract of property that includes present-day Pennsylvania. Penn intended to use the land to establish a colony in which the Religious Society of Friends, or Quakers, could practice their religious beliefs in freedom.

On March 4, 1681, King Charles II granted a land charter to William Penn as repayment of a loan he had received from Penn's father. The younger Penn proposed that the large tract of land should be called *Sylvania*, meaning woods in Latin. Charles II liked the idea, but thought the elder Penn should be honored by adding "Penn" to the beginning of the name.

The next day, William Penn wrote down some of his thoughts about the new colony that had just been given to him by the British Crown. Penn believed that God would make this colony "the seed of a nation."[23]

CHOOSING A NAME FOR THE COLONY

William Penn read descriptions of his newly acquired property in the New World. What he read reminded him of the landscape and weather of Wales, which at that time was an English province located in the southwestern part of the country. Wales is a mountainous region, boasting 14 mountains over 3,000 feet. The highest is Mount Snowdon, which reaches a height of 3,560 feet. After reading written descriptions of his colonial holdings, Penn could only relate it to Wales. Thus, he wanted to name the new colony "New Wales."

Penn suggested the name to King Charles II. Upon hearing of the request, Welsh members of Parliament protested, claiming the name of their homeland was too civilized and refined for such an untamed and rough place. Besides, the Welsh were loyal Christians under the British Crown and they did not wish to see the name of their region associated with a colony founded by Quakers.

Always the peacemaker, William Penn offered another name. Still drawing on the written descriptions of the forested land he had yet to visit, Penn proposed the name *Sylvania*, which is the Latin word meaning *woods*. Charles II liked the proposal, but decided to change it slightly, calling it *Pennsylvania*, or *Penn's Woods*. "Charles, who loved a word of double meaning," no doubt knew that Penn means *great* and *high*.[24] Thus, *Pennsylvania* also means *great and high woods*.

For his part, and true to his Quaker beliefs that frowned upon drawing attention to oneself, Penn cringed at the appearance of arrogance. However, the king assured Penn that the name was not meant to honor the holder of the colonial charter, but his father, Admiral Sir William Penn. Penn, however, then attempted to sidestep the king by offering a bribe of 20 guineas to the secretary completing the paperwork and signing the grant.[25] The secretary was a loyalist who knew that the king had named the land tract himself, and turned down the bribe. Penn, who had done all he could to avoid the appearance of conceit, was left to soothe his concerns in the fact the king had named the land for an old friend and naval hero—Admiral William Penn. Thus, despite Penn's concerns, the land on which the holy experiment was to take place was named Pennsylvania.

7

Penn Comes to America

Shortly after receiving his charter, William Penn decided to write those few European settlers already living in his colony. Dated April 8, 1681, Penn's letter reassured the colonists that he would be a kind and generous leader. He told them that they "shall be governed by laws of your own making."[26] He also wrote that he "shall not usurp the right of any, or oppress his person."[27] Penn wanted his colonists to know that he intended to build a colony in which religious differences would be tolerated, and the citizens could govern themselves. Once he arrived in America, Penn did his best to form a government in which the people ruled themselves. He also saw to it that individuals were allowed to worship freely.

A LONG AND DIFFICULT VOYAGE

Penn appointed William Markham, his first cousin, to serve as his deputy governor of Pennsylvania. Markham left for America in the summer of 1681. Before the end of the year, two ships filled with Quakers and supplies arrived in the new colony. Meanwhile, Penn prepared to go to America. He gave instructions to Markham through letters. He also sent letters to the Native Americans in Pennsylvania, reassuring them of his peaceful intentions. Markham was responsible for purchasing land, communicating Penn's ideals with the colonists, and establishing good relations with the Delaware, the local tribe. As Penn's representative, Markham demonstrated that the governor was a leader who cared for people.

Markham met with the Native Americans, and on behalf of Penn, asked if he could buy their land. Markham told them that Penn was "a just man who would neither do them wrong himself" nor allow others in the colony "to do them wrong."[28] Further, Penn wanted "to live with them in love; to buy their lands if he should want it; and to trade with them in open market, as a white man bought and sold with white men."[29] The Delawares were moved by such consideration for their feelings and sold Penn the parcel of land he wanted. In July, the price was agreed to, and the transaction took place in August 1681—more than a year before Penn even arrived in America.

Penn made all the necessary arrangements. He left his financial affairs in the hands of an aide, Philip Ford. Penn finally left England in the fall of 1682. Gulielma, his wife, was pregnant and unable to go with William, but the governor hoped his family could soon join him in America.

Penn faced a grueling journey onboard the *Welcome*. Around 100 passengers endured crowded conditions. After a few weeks at sea, the danger of disease appeared with an outbreak of smallpox. Penn, who survived the disease as a child, was apparently immune, but smallpox claimed the lives of about 30 people on the voyage. Finally, after two long months, the *Welcome* arrived in America.

In October 1682, William Penn arrived in his new colony at the point where the Delaware and Schuylkill rivers converge (near the site of what is today the Philadelphia Naval Yard). Many local residents, including Dutch, Germans, English, and Native Americans, gathered to greet the new governor.

A NEW KIND OF LEADER

It was a grand day in late October 1682. A crowd of people jostled one other for standing space at the primitive dock near the place where the Delaware and Schuylkill rivers converge. The throng was a collection of the local townspeople: Old people and young people were there; there were Dutch and English, as well as Germans and Swedes. The enthusiastic crowd had gathered to see a man come ashore from the ship docked near the bank. The man was William Penn, the new governor of a newly established colony that included the little town.

Rumors had spread throughout the town about the new governor. All were "eager to catch a glimpse of the man who was said to come amongst them, less as their lord and governor than as their friend."[30] The townspeople had come out in large numbers to see this man for themselves, this new kind of leader. Finally, he appeared and made his way to shore. The crowd greeted him warmly and enthusiastically. The throng pushed in to see and hear the man they had come to see, the man who was to be their new governor.

The following day, William Penn officially took over as governor. The day would be filled with formal ceremonies and a public gathering. Governor Penn assembled the townspeople together in the courthouse, which was built by some of the Dutch settlers. At this meeting, the new governor formally took possession of the colony. These formalities included the reading of charters and the presentation of deeds. Agents of James, Duke of York, who was brother and heir to King Charles II, were there, too. The Duke of York held legitimate claims to some of the lands now passing to Penn. To symbolize the transfer of ownership, the agents gave "earth and water" from the property in question.[31] These symbols date back to ancient times, when the conquering Persians demanded tokens of earth and water from conquered cities to represent Persian supremacy and rights to the land and all its products. Europeans continued the tradition, though the written documents carried more legal weight than did the token dirt and water. Penn graciously accepted these tokens, thereby sealing the deal. William Penn now legally owned a tract of land that later became the state of Pennsylvania, comprised of nearly 45,000 square miles of territory.

Then, the new governor spoke to those gathered. He told them why he came to the little settlement on the Delaware River. He shared with them his vision for establishing a "free and virtuous state in which the people should rule themselves."[32] He described the powers he held as governor, but he also qualified his remarks by declaring his intention to use his powers only in the short term, in order to benefit the colony—not himself.

Thus began William Penn's holy experiment—the founding of a colony in North America. This colony, called Pennsylvania, was unlike the other colonies. There was no official religion of the colony. No religious group held an advantage

PENN'S PLAN OF UNION

William Penn wrote many religious tracts and pamphlets concerning liberty and government. Perhaps his most visionary idea was a rather brief plan for unifying the English colonies in North America. In 1696, England and France were at war. Each had colonies in North America. Thus, their colonial holdings became part of the war effort. In England, the Board of Trade wanted to coordinate colonial defense efforts. The issue was raised of drafting colonial residents into a defensive colonial force. William Penn appeared before the board and offered what was called *A Plan of Union for the American Colonies*. Penn intended his proposal as a means of ensuring a sound defense against French aggression, but the ideas contained in his plan would instead later appear in the U.S. Constitution.

Penn argued that if the board was to require the colonies to supply a set number of troops, then the colonies should be allowed to meet together and determine for themselves the numbers supplied by each colony. This gathering, or congress, was to ensure that the colonies "be made more useful to the Crown and one another's peace and safety."* Under his plan, each colony would send two representatives to the meeting, and the congress would meet at least once a year. In times of war, meetings would be more frequent. In times of peace, and if the congress decided to, the meetings could be as much as two years apart.

Although the Board of Trade did not implement Penn's plan, the ideas contained within it continued to live on. Penn seemed to realize, in 1696, what no one before him (and few after him) understood: The colonies needed to share some of the powers the federal government held over them. Eighty years later, in Penn's city of Philadelphia, a group of representatives from the Thirteen Colonies met in such a congress. On July 4, 1776, that congress voted to accept the Declaration of Independence—in large part because Britain had refused to share power with the colonial governments.

---

* Frederick B. Tolles and E. Gordon Alderfer, eds. *The Witness of William Penn* (New York: The MacMillan Company, 1957), 136.

8

The Rise of Philadelphia

William Penn believed that his new city should reflect the values he held as a Quaker. He did not want government to simply rule over the people, but instead, be a reflection of the people. "When William Penn planned his colony on the Delaware, he had the amazing notion that he wanted his people to be governed in such a way that they would be happy."[35] This was a groundbreaking idea that had never been tried when Penn established the city of Philadelphia. But the leader's personal experiences of suffering at the hands of the government for his religious convictions convinced him that a just government needed to protect individual religious liberty. When Penn made plans for his colony and its capital, he maintained his principles of individual rights and self-government.

POPULATING A COLONIAL CITY

Before leaving for the New World, William Penn advertised in England that he intended to establish on the banks of the Delaware River, "a large Towne."[36] From these advertisements, many people decided to move to America, to live in Penn's colony. Many of these colonists were religious people who disagreed with the Church of England. Quakers, Catholics, and other religious minorities made plans to go to Pennsylvania. Penn's holy experiment was beginning to attract people to America.

He also aimed to live in peace with the local Native Americans. Thus, Philadelphia, unlike many of the other early settlements, had neither walls nor soldiers. Penn's treatment of the Native Americans further reinforced his attitude of living in peace with all others.

WILLIAM PENN AND THE LENNI LENAPE

Amazingly, early biographers of Penn recognized the unique approach the founder took in dealing with the natives. According to one author, Penn's biographers "in seven languages and seven lands, unanimously extol his relations with the Indians as one of his greatest achievements" in establishing Pennsylvania.[37] Another states, "He will always be mentioned with honour as the founder of a colony, who did not, in his dealings with a savage people, abuse the strength derived from civilizations."[38] For Penn, the question of how to treat the Native Americans was not an issue: He simply believed it was his duty as a Quaker to treat them fairly. "Penn's entire treatment of the Indians was based on his conception of them as fellow-sons of God, to be treated by him as brothers."[39]

Penn negotiated nine different treaties with the Native Americans from 1682–1684. Through these meetings, the governor pledged his friendship. He also purchased land from them. In this regard, Penn was true to his convictions. The governor did not simply take land from the Native Americans. He believed the land was rightfully his, given by Charles II, but "his deep sense of humanity made him realize the importance of the Indians, as children of God, and brothers."[40]

Between 1682 and 1684, William Penn negotiated nine different treaties with the Delaware, or Lenni Lenape, Indians. Penn gained the trust of the original inhabitants of Pennsylvania by learning their language and customs and treating them with respect.

Each time he met with the natives, Penn was careful to observe their customs and treat them with respect. Usually, the two sides began their meeting by participating in a tribal custom together. This custom was the ritual smoking of a peace pipe, or calumet. Penn observed the Native American tradition of discussing peace, then discussing the main topic, which was usually land. After speaking about peace, it was then acceptable to bring up the subject of land.

As discussed earlier, after Penn made his request, the Native Americans met by themselves to discuss the proposal. Their leaders talked while Penn and other settlers waited patiently. Penn understood that each chief needed an opportunity to consider the issue.

BROTHER ONAS

Perhaps the greatest tribute bestowed on William Penn by the tribes living in Pennsylvania was the name they gave him— Onas. The Native Americans knew that the white men wrote with a quill feather, called a pen. The Lenni Lenape name for such a writing instrument was *onas*, which meant quill or pen. The Native Americans heard the governor's last name and afterward referred to him by his Indian name, Onas.

Onas was a good friend to the Native Americans. When he made promises to them, he kept his word. He did not take their lands from them. He treated them as if they were members of his own family. Because of his love and friendship, they respected Penn. They called him *Brother Onas*, to show that they loved and accepted him. For the governor and his new friends, whose relationship began with a letter promising friendship, the pen was indeed mightier than the sword.

A SHINING CITY

William Penn excitedly made plans for the capital city for his colony. After careful deliberation, he chose a site located at the junction of two rivers, the Delaware and Schuylkill. Others wanted Chester, Pennsylvania's oldest city located farther downstream on the Delaware River, to hold this honor, but Penn and

THE LIBERTY BELL

One of Philadelphia's most familiar symbols is the Liberty Bell. In 1751, the Pennsylvania Assembly commissioned the bell to celebrate the 50-year anniversary of Pennsylvania's original constitution. William Penn wrote the document in 1701. He called it the Charter of Privileges. In his charter, Penn emphasized the importance of individual rights and liberties.

The bell includes a reference to a passage in the Bible: Leviticus 25:10, which states, "And ye shall hallow the fiftieth year, and *proclaim liberty throughout all the land unto all the inhabitants thereof*" (the bell is inscribed with the italicized portion). The year 1751 marked 50 years since Penn had issued his charter. The Pennsylvania Assembly speaker, a Quaker named Isaac Norris, chose the fitting passage.

The bell was made in London and shipped to Philadelphia in 1752. It was hung on March 10, 1753, when it cracked the first time it was rung. Some believed the bell was too brittle, and two local foundry workers, John Pass and John Stow, melted down the bell and recast it with more copper added to it. Many objected to the new bell, claiming it had too much copper. Pass and Snow again recast the bell. This bell, weighing 2,080 pounds, was hung on June 11, 1753, in the steeple of the Pennsylvania statehouse (now called Independence Hall).

Some were still displeased with this third version of the bell, but when a fourth arrived from England, Norris believed it sounded no better than the one already hanging at the statehouse. Thus, the bell stayed where it was until it was removed for safekeeping during the Revolutionary War. Few agree when the recognizable crack began to form, but all agree that it reached its current state when the bell was rung in celebration of Washington's birthday in 1846. Today, the bell is silent, but the message of liberty etched on it speaks loudly.

his surveyor, Thomas Holme, disagreed. The two decided that the land located so near two navigable rivers provided the best opportunities for future growth. This place, known as Wiccacoa, was a small peninsula, positioned between the two rivers. The Schuylkill fed into the Delaware and Penn chose the land near this confluence as the site of his great city.

The Liberty Bell was constructed in 1751 to commemorate the fiftieth anniversary of Pennsylvania's original constitution. The motto—"Proclaim liberty throughout all the land unto all the inhabitants thereof"—is visible at the top of the bell.

There were many other advantages unique to the place. Good land was abundant, with no swampy marshlands to overcome. Rich clay was plentiful, which came in handy for making bricks. Equally important, large rock quarries were within just a few miles. Some of these quarries even held white marble. And, of course, access to the river was easy and protected by the high banks. Penn had sought the perfect place for his chief city, and he had found it.

After having selected the site, Penn set about purchasing land. Three Swedish settlers owned the property. Although it was within Penn's rights to simply lay claim to the land, he acted with respect toward the Swedes. He approached them and told them of his intent to buy the land from them. The Swedes named their price, and Penn paid it. Having completed the necessary steps to obtain the land, Penn enthusiastically began to draw up plans.

The governor left little to chance as he sketched out his ideas for his city. Penn did not want the city to grow randomly. Instead, he made plans for a city much larger than others thought possible. He had a bold vision for what the city could and would later become. He laid out a city with four sections. At the center of the city were 10 acres of unspoiled land set aside for common use. Likewise, each of the four sections also included an eight-acre plot set aside for all to use then and in the future. Penn dreamed of Philadelphia becoming "a green country town."[41]

The city was to occupy 12 square miles. Streets were plotted to run east-west and north-south. More importantly, the streets were at least 50-feet wide, and some were 100-feet wide—wider than any streets in London at the time. To keep things simple, Penn numbered the streets running north-south and named the east-west streets, most of them after types of trees found in the area.

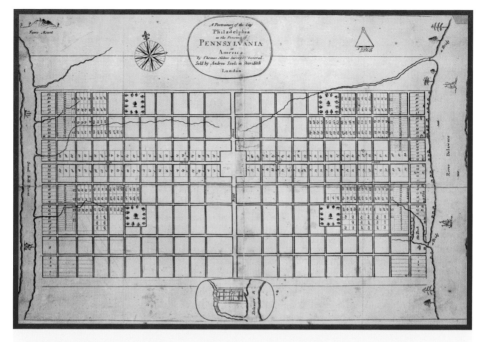

When William Penn planned the design of Philadelphia, he set out to create a city that would be split into four sections, with a 10-acre park in the middle. In addition, the city's original north-south streets were numbered, while the east-west streets were largely named after trees native to the area.

A brick and timber-framed building that served several functions was the first nonresidential building constructed. In its day, it was a magnificent building, called the Blue Anchor. The structure was made with bricks imported from England, and featured large timber frames. One side of the building abutted the river. The other extended into what later became Dock Street. The Blue Anchor was perfectly situated to become the early center of business activity in Philadelphia. Located on the river, the Blue Anchor was a tavern, a gathering place, a docking station, and an all-purpose trading place. Local residents went there to see others and drink with them. The building also served as the local post office.

Just a few months later, Penn happily released updated figures of his fledgling city. Merchants had moved to Philadelphia. The new city had attracted artisans of all trades. Nearby lands were already cleared and put to use as farms. The formerly small village boasted 80 homes. Penn unblushingly beamed to a friend, "I must without vanity say, I have led the greatest colony into America that ever any man did on private credit."[42] Indeed, Penn had every right to delight in his undertaking. One year to the day after Penn landed in the New World, residents in Philadelphia had built 100 houses. Two years later, the number of houses soared to 600. Penn claimed the city's population in 1684 was 2,500. Others claimed a population of 12,000 in 1697. However, some historians dispute the city was quite that large that soon, calling the population claims "greatly exaggerated."[43] Regardless, all agree that the city grew quickly.

Houses began to spring up all across the city. The early Swedish settlers lived in log homes, built with notched wood and without nails. The English colonists, however, built homes similar to the ones they had in England. Thus, the English residents began building homes made of "wood frame and brick construction," much like the Blue Anchor.[44] By 1690, the residents built enough out of bricks that there were four brick makers and 10 bricklayers. Philadelphia was growing into the city Penn envisioned.

AN UNEXPECTED ABSENCE

In 1684, William Penn learned that the land he purchased from the Duke of York might be lost. The Maryland charter, dating back to 1632, seemed to include Philadelphia. Penn tried to meet with the proprietor of Maryland, Lord Baltimore, in order to settle the dispute. However, Lord Baltimore went to England to plead his case before the king's privy council. Penn believed that he needed to be present in England to protect his colony and city of brotherly love.

Penn prepared to return to England. He left directions for the construction of gardens, walkways, riverside steps, and other improvements to be made at Pennsbury. Then, certain that his trip to England would be brief, he left his beloved Pennsylvania. He did not know that events would keep him away from America for 15 years.

9

Philadelphia Since 1701

When William Penn returned to England, he found King Charles II in declining health. Charles had sent Parliament home and was ruling much like an absolute monarch. For Penn, the situation could not have been much worse—Charles seemed uninterested in the American colonies. Instead of a speedy hearing and decision, Penn faced the likelihood that a resolution to the boundary dispute might take years. Just four months after Penn's arrival in England, Charles II died. His brother and practicing Catholic, James II, became king.

At first, James helped move the border dispute closer to a final decision. The privy council, at James's urging, split Delaware between the two colonies. Penn received the eastern portion beside the Delaware River. Lord Baltimore received the western portion located on the Chesapeake Bay. This was the primary area of disagreement, and the decision allowed each colony to continue growing. However, the settlement only partially solved the dispute. Penn decided to remain in England until the matter was completely settled.

A NEW KING

Unfortunately, James did not rule wisely. The king did little to keep the peace or to calm fears that he might force England to become Catholic. Most in Parliament were willing to overlook his faults, because he had no male heir. Besides, James's daughter Mary was next in line to the throne, and both she and her husband, William of Orange, were committed Protestants. However, James and his second wife then had a child, a boy. England suddenly faced the likelihood of a line of Catholic kings.

A revolt broke out, and Parliament invited William and Mary to rule England. Support for James withered. Eventually, the king had to flee to France. William and Mary signed the English Bill of Rights, which guaranteed the power of Parliament over the king. The Glorious Revolution ended, and William and Mary had become king and queen.

William Penn was now an outsider. Whereas before he was a personal friend to the king, now he was a possible traitor. After all, the former king now lived in exile. Penn feared he might completely lose Pennsylvania. Penn decided to return to America, but the political tensions prevented it. James plotted to recapture his throne, and Penn's close ties with him caused others to mistrust him. Penn was arrested three different times and placed in prison. He finally decided to retire to his country home and wait for the suspicions to pass.

In 1692, William and Mary seized Pennsylvania and declared it a royal colony. Penn pled his case before the king, trying to demonstrate his loyalty to the throne. In February 1694, Penn's wife Gulielma died. The founder grieved, but word soon reached him that William and Mary had issued him a new charter. Penn was receiving his colony for a second time!

In 1696, 52-year-old William Penn married his second wife, 24-year-old Hannah Callowhill, at the Friends' meetinghouse in Bristol, England. After William's death in 1718, Hannah served as acting proprietor of Pennsylvania until she died eight years later.

Penn wanted to return to America and live in his colony. Before leaving, though, the 52-year-old Penn married for a second time in 1696. His new wife was 24-year-old Hannah Callowhill.

PENN RETURNS TO AMERICA

Penn arrived in Philadelphia on December 1, 1699. The next January, Hannah gave birth to a son, John—Penn's only child born in America. While in Pennsylvania, Penn did all he could to help the colony grow. He again met with local Native Americans, much as he had in 1682–1684. More importantly, Penn continued to protect the religious rights of Quakers and others. Many Anglicans had moved into the colony, and now Quakers feared they might face persecution.

The governor acted on those founding principles he had always believed in: namely, that the people ought to be able to govern themselves. Penn wrote the Frame of Government of Pennsylvania, the fourth version of the colony's constitution. Each of the others was in effect for a short period of time. However, the fourth frame, the Charter of Privileges, was offered and accepted in 1701. Amazingly, Penn gave up powers to the assembly under the charter. This constitution remained in effect until the Declaration of Independence in 1776, when Pennsylvania ratified a new state constitution. Of course, the religious rights and powers of self-government continued under the new constitution.

Shortly after the adoption of the Charter of Privileges, Penn decided he needed to return again to England. Some of his enemies had complained to the king about his handling of Pennsylvania. Rather than fight the charges from a distance, the governor chose to argue his case in person. Thus, in November 1701, Penn, his wife, and young son left America. William Penn never again saw his holy experiment.

BACK TO ENGLAND

When William Penn left his beloved Philadelphia in 1701, he fully intended to return to the city. However, events outside his control prevented his return. Soon after he arrived in England, the primary threat to him disappeared. William died, and Queen Anne (Mary's sister) came to the throne in 1702 (Mary died in 1694). She believed in tolerance, and there was no more talk of taking away colonies from proprietors.

However, a greater threat now emerged. Penn's trusted aide Philip Ford had used his position to put Penn in debt. Ford claimed that Penn owed him some £10,000, a huge amount! Penn had trusted Ford, and had often signed paperwork from Ford without reading it carefully. Now these papers with his signature were used against him. The Fords took Penn to court, where he was ordered to pay. In January 1708, Penn was placed in debtor's prison. Eventually, the Fords and Penn settled their suit out of court, and Penn won his release.

Lacking the funds to return to Pennsylvania, William Penn retired to a country home outside London. There he promoted the Quaker cause and kept in contact with his agents in America. However, he suffered a debilitating stroke in 1712. Following the stroke, Penn was unable to care for himself. After lingering for six more years, William Penn died in 1718. But his dream for a colony founded upon the ideal of self-government lived on. As one historian stated, "His experiment was to bear witness to the world that there is in human nature virtue for self-government."[45]

COLONIAL AND REVOLUTIONARY PHILADELPHIA

Throughout the eighteenth century, Philadelphia continued to grow. The city served as a major political center. When tensions arose between the colonies and England, Philadelphia—which was centrally located in the colonies—became the site of the First and Second Continental Congresses. The First Continental Congress effectively organized a boycott of English goods in response to Parliament's actions against the colonies for the Boston Tea Party. The Second Continental Congress formed an army to defend the colonies, appointing George Washington its commander. On July 4, 1776, the Congress declared the colonies independent from England. The body also served as the new government until the Articles of Confederation was ratified in 1781. Then, the Second Continental Congress adjourned, but

Philadelphia served as the headquarters for the Second Continental Congress from 1775 to 1781. The body of representatives from each of the 13 American colonies included Benjamin Franklin, John Adams, and Thomas Jefferson, who are depicted here (left to right) reviewing a draft of the Declaration of Independence.

it reconvened the very next day as the Confederation Congress. Philadelphia saw the birth of the new nation.

In 1787, Philadelphia again served host to a group of representatives. This time, the group met to amend the Articles

BENJAMIN FRANKLIN: THE ESSENCE OF PENN'S DREAM

One of the most remarkable Americans of the eighteenth century was a man who called Philadelphia his home: Benjamin Franklin. The future diplomat and inventor was born in Boston in 1706. At age 17, Franklin left home and moved to Philadelphia. From there, he later went to London, where he learned the printing trade. He returned to Philadelphia in 1726, engaged in printing, and managed to own his own printing house by 1730. He published a newspaper, *The Pennsylvania Gazette*. But it was his *Poor Richard's Almanack* that helped make him famous. The *Almanack* included many sayings, and Franklin sold about 10,000 copies a year. Franklin made a nice living as a publisher and earned the respect of others.

Franklin also had a knack for inventing things that people needed. Some of his ideas became the lightning rod, bifocal glasses, even a wood-burning stove (the Franklin stove). The inventor turned revolutionary when England began pressing its will on the American colonies. Franklin served as a representative for Pennsylvania in London until 1775. Then, he returned to America and was promptly elected to represent Pennsylvania in the Second Continental Congress. He and John Adams served together on a committee and helped edit Thomas Jefferson's draft of the Declaration of Independence. During the Revolutionary War, Franklin acted as commissioner to France, where he helped secure French recognition of the new nation. The treaty he negotiated provided much-needed funding for the American war effort. After the war, Franklin attended the 1787 convention in Philadelphia that produced the U.S. Constitution. He died in 1790.

But it is Franklin's apparent lack of religious commitment that helps define him as the essence of Penn's dream. The talented printer was able to live out his dreams, yet did not conform to many of the religious beliefs of the day. William Penn no doubt would have been proud that Philadelphia served as home to one of the most interesting and well-known Americans of the eighteenth century: Benjamin Franklin—printer, inventor, scientist, diplomat, public figure, and religious nonconformist.

of Confederation. Instead, the 55 men wrote an entirely new document, the U.S. Constitution. The new constitution was soon ratified, and the United States of America elected George Washington its first president. In the spring of 1789, George

Although he was born in Boston, Benjamin Franklin became one of Philadelphia's most famous residents. In addition to his many inventions, including bifocal eyeglasses and the lightning rod, Franklin was also responsible for establishing the first hospital and library in the colonies.

Washington became the first to take the presidential oath of office. At that time, New York City served as the national capital. The next year, as part of a compromise hammered out by Alexander Hamilton and Thomas Jefferson, the federal government relocated to Philadelphia. Thus, Penn's capital city became the seat of government for the new nation that was founded by the people. William Penn's dream for a successful self-government had become a reality. In 1800, the federal government moved again, this time to an unfinished city—Washington, D.C.

NINETEENTH-CENTURY PHILADELPHIA

Throughout the nineteenth century, Philadelphia continued to grow. It remained the second-largest city in the United States until 1830, when Baltimore surpassed it. In 1800, two of Philadelphia's suburbs—Northern Liberties and Southwark, now part of Philadelphia—ranked sixth and seventh. Thus, greater Philadelphia was the largest metropolitan city in America in the early years of the nation.

In 1854, the city of Philadelphia expanded its boundaries to include all of Philadelphia County. The extension included Germantown and other smaller communities, as well as the inclusion of areas of modern Philadelphia: Northeast Philadelphia, North Philadelphia, South Philadelphia, and West Philadelphia.

Philadelphia aided the emergence of the steam locomotive in America. The city served as one of the early railroad centers. Penn's city was ideally situated to serve as a channel between shipping from the Delaware River and railroads to the interior. The Baldwin Locomotive Works originally made Philadelphia its base of operations, although the company later moved to Eddystone, Pennsylvania. At one time, the Pennsylvania Railroad was the largest railroad by revenue and volume of traffic in the country. (Located in Philadelphia, the Pennsylvania

Railroad later gained fame as one of four railroads included in the board game Monopoly.) The company later merged with Penn Central, and today is owned by Conrail, which is still headquartered in Philadelphia.

In 1876, a special honor was accorded Philadelphia. That year, Philadelphia became the first American city to host the World's Fair. The event was called the Centennial Exposition to commemorate the 100-year anniversary of the signing of the Declaration of Independence. Philadelphia's fair featured several noteworthy displays: Alexander Graham Bell's telephone, Heinz ketchup (a Pennsylvania product), and Hires root beer, invented by a Philadelphia pharmacist. Memorial Hall and the mall in front of it are modern reminders of Philadelphia's Centennial Exposition.

MODERN PHILADELPHIA

As the twentieth century dawned, Philadelphia continued as a regional and national center. The city celebrated the 150-year anniversary of the Declaration of Independence in 1926, and it continued to grow throughout the first half of the twentieth century. Then, after 1950, the city's population began to decline. The city reached its height in 1950, when it boasted 2.07 million people. Then, its population began to drop. Despite the loss of population, Philadelphia today is the fifth-largest U.S. city, with a population of more than 1.5 million people. The Philadelphia metropolitan area is composed of more than 5.7 million people, and is the fourth-largest metropolitan area in the United States.

WILLIAM PENN'S LEGACY

Today, Pennsylvania's founder would probably not recognize his beloved Philadelphia. Despite the enormous growth of his city of brotherly love, Penn would no doubt delight in how many of his ideas are woven into the fabric of American life. For example, his belief in religious freedom is found within the First Amendment; his ideas of self-government are found in the U.S. Constitution and in each of the 50 state constitutions; his novel approach to shared power is seen in the U.S. system of checks and balances between the branches of government; his insistence on jury rights is now safeguarded in the Sixth Amendment; and his pacifist convictions have been adopted and imitated by men such as India's Mahatma Gandhi and Martin Luther King, Jr., both of whom waged their own struggles for individual rights. William Penn's holy experiment helped shape the United States into the nation it is today. The city of Philadelphia stands as a lasting monument to a Quaker who dreamed of a better life— William Penn, the founder of Pennsylvania.

Chronology

1492 Genoan Christopher Columbus, sailing for Spain, "discovers" the New World.

1497 Genoan John Cabot becomes the first early modern European to explore North America's northeastern coast.

1558 Elizabeth I ascends to the throne of England.

1603 Elizabeth I dies, and is succeeded by her Scottish cousin, James Stuart.

1607 The English establish their first permanent colony at Jamestown, Virginia.

1625 James I dies and is succeeded by his son Charles I.

1632 George Calvert receives a charter for the Maryland Colony, which includes the future site of Philadelphia; however, the Maryland Colony never extends control to the area.

1643 Swedish colonists become the first Europeans to settle in the area near modern-day Philadelphia, as part of the New Sweden Colony; later, the Dutch incorporate the Swedish colony into New Netherland, which later falls into the hands of England.

1644 William Penn is born in London, England.

1649 King Charles I is beheaded.

1653–58 Oliver Cromwell rules England as Lord Protector.

1656 The Penn family goes into exile in Ireland.

1657 William Penn hears the Quaker preacher Thomas Loe.

1658 Oliver Cromwell dies.

1660 Charles II, son of Charles I, is crowned king; William Penn attends Oxford.

1667 William Penn becomes a Quaker; a year later, he loses his inheritance for his beliefs.

1672 William Penn marries Gulielma Springett.

1680 Penn petitions Charles II for a land grant as payment for a debt the king still owed the Penn family.

1681 On March 1, King Charles II grants a land charter to William Penn for a large tract that includes what is now Pennsylvania.

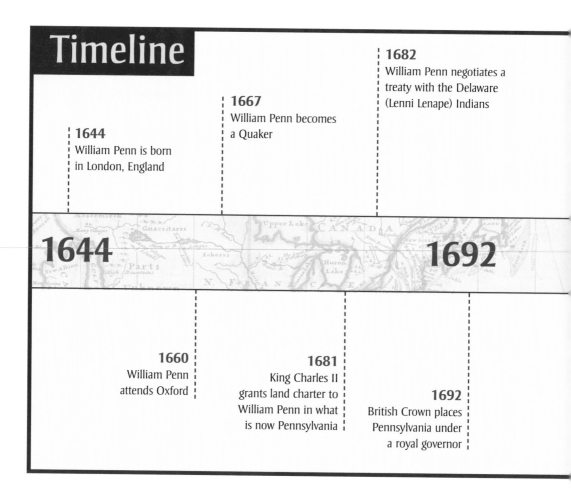

Timeline

1644
William Penn is born in London, England

1667
William Penn becomes a Quaker

1682
William Penn negotiates a treaty with the Delaware (Lenni Lenape) Indians

1644   **1692**

1660
William Penn attends Oxford

1681
King Charles II grants land charter to William Penn in what is now Pennsylvania

1692
British Crown places Pennsylvania under a royal governor

1682 William Penn negotiates a treaty with the Delaware (Lenni Lenape) Indians from the Shackamaxon village.

1685 Charles II dies and his brother James II becomes king.

1688 Pennsylvania Quakers are the first to protest against slavery in the English colonies.

1688–89 William and Mary jointly ascend to the throne in the Glorious Revolution, after Mary's father, James II, flees England.

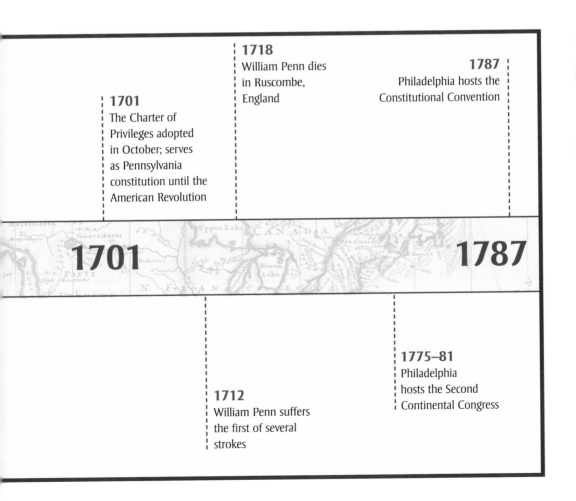

1718
William Penn dies in Ruscombe, England

1787
Philadelphia hosts the Constitutional Convention

1701
The Charter of Privileges adopted in October; serves as Pennsylvania constitution until the American Revolution

1701

1787

1775–81
Philadelphia hosts the Second Continental Congress

1712
William Penn suffers the first of several strokes

1692 Penn is stripped of all powers over Pennsylvania when the Crown places the colony under a royal governor.

1694 Penn regains all powers over the Pennsylvania Colony; Penn's wife Gulielma dies.

1696 Penn marries Hannah Callowhill.

1699 William Penn returns to Pennsylvania for a second time, arriving in Philadelphia on December 1.

1701 The Charter of Privileges is adopted in October, serving as the Pennsylvania constitution until the American Revolution; William Penn leaves his beloved colony for the last time, and returns to England.

1712 William Penn suffers the first of several strokes; he is incapacitated for the rest of his life.

1718 William Penn dies in Ruscombe, England; his body is buried in a Quaker cemetery at Jordans, Buckinghamshire.

1751 The Pennsylvania Assembly commissions a bell made to celebrate the 50-year anniversary of William Penn's Charter of Privileges.

1753 The Liberty Bell is displayed at the Pennsylvania Statehouse.

1775–81 Philadelphia hosts the Second Continental Congress in which the 13 colonies issue the Declaration of Independence.

1787 Philadelphia hosts the Constitutional Convention.

Notes

Chapter 1

1. Hepworth W. Dixon, *A History of William Penn: Founder of Pennsylvania* (New York: New Amsterdam Book Company, 1902), 199.
2. As condensed in Genevieve Foster, *The World of William Penn* (New York: Charles Scribner's Sons, 1973), 45.
3. Quoted in Charles F. Jenkins and the William Penn Tercentary Committee, compilers, *Remember William Penn, 1644–1944: A Tercentary Memorial* (Harrisburg, Pa.: Commonwealth of Pennsylvania, 1945), 120.
4. Ibid., 113.
5. Dixon, 202.
6. Foster, 48.

Chapter 2

7. Clayton Roberts and David Roberts, *A History of England* (2 vols.) (Englewood Cliffs, N.J.: Prentice-Hall, 1985), 1.
8. Ibid.

Chapter 3

9. Thomas J. Archdeacon, *New York City, 1644–1710: Conquest and Change* (London: Cornell University Press, 1976), 36.

Chapter 4

10. Jenkins, 3.
11. William I. Hull, *William Penn: A Topical Biography* (London: Oxford University Press, 1937), 183.

Chapter 5

12. Dixon, 97.
13. Ibid., 101.
14. Ibid., 103.
15. Ibid., 103–104.
16. Ibid., 105.
17. Ibid.
18. Ibid., 106.
19. Ibid.
20. Hull, 24.

Chapter 6

21. Joseph J. Kelley, Jr. *Life and Times in Colonial Philadelphia* (Harrisburg, Pa.: Stackpole Books, 1973), 30.
22. Dixon, 136.
23. Jean R. Soderlund, *William Penn and the Founding of Pennsylvania, 1680–1684: A Documentary History* (Philadelphia: The University of Pennsylvania Press, 1983), 3.
24. Dixon, 177.
25. Ibid., 178.

Chapter 7

26. Soderlund, 55.
27. Ibid.
28. Dixon, 184.
29. Ibid., 184–185.
30. Ibid., 193.
31. Ibid.
32. Ibid.
33. Ibid, 169.
34. Ibid, 172.

Chapter 8

35. John T. Faris, *The Romance of Old Philadelphia* (Philadelphia and London: J.B. Lippincott Company, 1918), 66.
36. Richard S. Dunn and Mary Maples Dunn, eds. *The World of William Penn* (Philadelphia: University of Pennsylvania Press, 1986), 1.
37. Hull, 330.
38. Hull, 330 and Jenkins, 111.
39. Jenkins, 112.
40. Ibid., 109.
41. Dixon, 205.
42. Ibid., 207.
43. Russell F. Weigley, ed. Nicholas B. Wainwright and Edwin Wolf II, associate eds. *Philadelphia: A 300-Year History* (New York: W.W. Norton & Company, 1982), 11.
44. Ibid.

Chapter 9

45. Dixon, 16.

Bibliography

Archdeacon, Thomas J. *New York City, 1644–1710: Conquest and Change*. Ithaca, N.Y.: Cornell University Press, 1976.

Barbour, Hugh S., ed. *William Penn on Religion and Ethics: The Emergence of Liberal Quakerism* (2 vols.). Lewiston, N.Y.: The Edwin Mellen Press, 1991.

Buck, William J. *William Penn in America or An Account of His Life*. Philadelphia: Printed for the Author, 1888.

Clarkson, Thomas. *Memoirs of the Private and Public Life of William Penn*. Manchester, England: Bradshaw and Blacklock Printers, 1849.

Comfort, William Wistar. *William Penn and Our Liberties*. Philadelphia: The Penn Mutual Life Insurance Company, 1947.

Dixon, W. Hepworth. *A History of William Penn: Founder of Pennsylvania*. New York: New Amsterdam Book Company, 1902.

Dunn, Richard S., and Mary Maples Dunn, eds. *The World of William Penn*. Philadelphia: University of Pennsylvania Press, 1986.

Durland, William. *William Penn, James Madison and the Historical Crisis in American Federalism*. Lewiston, N.Y.: The Edwin Mellen Press, 2000.

Faris, John T. *The Romance of Old Philadelphia*. Philadelphia and London: J.B. Lippincott, 1918.

Foster, Genevieve. *The World of William Penn*. New York: Charles Scribner's Sons, 1973.

Hull, William I. *William Penn: A Topical Biography*. London: Oxford University Press, 1937.

Jenkins, Charles F., and the William Penn Tercentenary Committee, comps. *Remember William Penn, 1644–1944: A Tercentary Memorial*. Harrisburg, Pa.: Commonwealth of Pennsylvania, 1945.

Kelley, Jr., Joseph J. *Life and Times in Colonial Philadelphia*. Harrisburg, Pa.: Stackpole Books, 1973.

Murphy, Andrew R. *The Political Writings of William Penn*. Indianapolis: Liberty Fund, 2002.

Roberts, Clayton, and David Roberts. *A History of England* (2 vols.). Englewood Cliffs, N.J.: Prentice-Hall, 1985.

Soderlund, Jean R., ed. *William Penn and the Founding of Pennsylvania, 1680–1684: A Documentary History*. Philadelphia: University of Pennsylvania Press, 1983.

Tolles, Frederick B., and E. Gordon Alderfer, eds. *The Witness of William Penn*. New York: The Macmillan Company, 1957.

Tully, Alan. *William Penn's Legacy: Politics and Social Structure in Provincial Pennsylvania, 1726–1755*. Baltimore: The Johns Hopkins University Press, 1977.

Weigley, Russell F., ed., and Nicholas B. Wainwright and Edwin Wolf II, associate eds. *Philadelphia: A 300-Year History*. New York: W.W. Norton & Company, 1982.

Further Reading

Comfort, William Wistar. *William Penn 1644–1718: A Tercentenary Estimate*. Philadelphia: University of Pennsylvania Press, 1944.

Dunn, Mary Maples, and Richard S. Dunn, eds. *The Papers of William Penn, Volume One (1644–1679)*. Philadelphia: University of Pennsylvania Press, 1981.

Lutz, Norma Jean. *William Penn: Founder of Democracy*. Philadelphia: Chelsea House Publishers, 2000.

Myers, Albert Cook, ed. *William Penn's Own Account of the Lenni Lenape or Delaware Indians*. Somerset, N.J.: The Middle Atlantic Press, 1970.

Penn, William. *My Irish Journal*. Edited by Isabel Grubb. London: Longmans, Green and Co., 1952.

———, and Joseph Besse, ed. *The Peace of Europe: The Fruits of Solitude and other Writings by William Penn*. London: J.M. Dent & Sons, 1915.

Web sites

William Penn—Some Fruits of Solitude
http://www.bartleby.com/1/3/

The Online Library of Liberty—William Penn
http://oll.libertyfund.org/Home3/Author.php?recordID=0464

Pennsbury Manor
http://www.pennsburymanor.org/PennInPa.html

The Quaker Province
http://www.phmc.state.pa.us/bah/pahist/quaker.asp?secid=31

The Religious Society of Friends
http://www.quaker.org/

Penn's Plan of Union
http://teachingamericanhistory.org/library/index.asp?document=969

Charter for the Province of Pennsylvania
http://www.yale.edu/lawweb/avalon/states/pa01.htm

Picture Credits

Index

About the Contributors

Series editor **TIM MCNEESE** is associate professor of history at York College in York, Nebraska, where he is in his fifteenth year of college instruction. Professor McNeese earned an Associate of Arts degree from York College, a Bachelor of Arts in history and political science from Harding University, and a Master of Arts in history from Missouri State University. A prolific author of books for elementary, middle and high school, and college readers, McNeese has published more than 80 books and educational materials over the past 20 years, on everything from Picasso to landmark Supreme Court decisions. His writing has earned him a citation in the library reference work *Contemporary Authors*. In 2006, McNeese appeared on the History Channel program *Risk Takers/History Makers: John Wesley Powell and the Grand Canyon*.

Author **SHANE MOUNTJOY** lives in York, Nebraska, where he is associate professor of history at York College. Professor Mountjoy holds an Associate of Arts degree from York College, a Bachelor of Arts degree from Lubbock Christian University, a Master of Arts from the University of Nebraska-Lincoln, and a Doctor of Philosophy from the University of Missouri-Columbia. He and his wife, Vivian, home-school their four daughters. A teacher and lover of history, geography, and political science, Mountjoy has written and edited more than 10 books.